MOVIE FAVORITES

Solos and String Orchestra Arrangements
Correlated with Essential Elements String Method

Arranged by
ELLIOT DEL BORGO

Welcome to Essential Elements Movie Favorites! There are two versions of each selection in this versatile book. The SOLO version appears in the beginning of your book. The STRING ORCHESTRA arrangements of each song follows. The supplemental CD recording or string orchestra PIANO PART may be used as an accompaniment for solo performance. Use these recordings when playing solos for friends and family.

ISBN 978-0-7935-8422-2

HAL•LEONARD®
CORPORATION
7777 W. BLUEMOUND RD. P.O. BOX 13819 MILWAUKEE, WI 53213

Copyright © 1999 by HAL LEONARD CORPORATION
International Copyright Secured   All Rights Reserved

00868023
2nd Edition

From CHARIOTS OF FIRE

CHARIOTS OF FIRE

STRING BASS
Solo

Music by VANGELIS
Arranged by ELLIOT DEL BORGO

00868023

From the Paramount Motion Picture FORREST GUMP

FORREST GUMP-MAIN TITLE
(Feather Theme)

STRING BASS
Solo

Music by ALAN SILVESTRI
Arranged by ELLIOT DEL BORGO

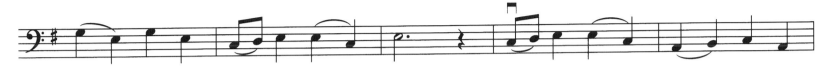

00868023

From APOLLO 13

APOLLO 13

(End Credits)

STRING BASS
Solo

By JAMES HORNER
Arranged by ELLIOT DEL BORGO

00868023

From DANCES WITH WOLVES

THE JOHN DUNBAR THEME

By JOHN BARRY
Arranged by ELLIOT DEL BORGO

STRING BASS
Solo

00868023

6

THEME FROM E.T.
(The Extra-Terrestrial)

STRING BASS
Solo

Music by **JOHN WILLIAMS**
Arranged by **ELLIOT DEL BORGO**

00868023

From the Universal Motion Picture JURASSIC PARK

THEME FROM "JURASSIC PARK"

STRING BASS
Solo

Composed by JOHN WILLIAMS
Arranged by ELLIOT DEL BORGO

00868023

From THE MAN FROM SNOWY RIVER

THE MAN FROM SNOWY RIVER
(Main Title Theme)

STRING BASS
Solo

By BRUCE ROWLAND
Arranged by ELLIOT DEL BORGO

From the Paramount Motion Picture MISSION: IMPOSSIBLE

MISSION: IMPOSSIBLE THEME

By LALO SCHIFRIN
Arranged by ELLIOT DEL BORGO

STRING BASS
Solo

From the Paramount Motion Picture RAIDERS OF THE LOST ARK

RAIDERS MARCH

STRING BASS
Solo

Music by JOHN WILLIAMS
Arranged by ELLIOT DEL BORGO

00868023

From AN AMERICAN TAIL

SOMEWHERE OUT THERE

STRING BASS
Solo

Words and Music by JAMES HORNER,
BARRY MANN and CYNTHIA WEIL
Arranged by ELLIOT DEL BORGO

MCA MUSIC PUBLISHING

00868023

Theme from the Paramount Picture STAR TREK: THE MOTION PICTURE

STAR TREK® THE MOTION PICTURE

STRING BASS
Solo

Music by JERRY GOLDSMITH
Arranged by ELLIOT DEL BORGO

CHARIOTS OF FIRE

STRING BASS
String Orchestra Arrangement

Music by VANGELIS
Arranged by ELLIOT DEL BORGO

From the Paramount Motion Picture FORREST GUMP

FORREST GUMP-MAIN TITLE

(Feather Theme)

STRING BASS
String Orchestra Arrangement

Music by ALAN SILVESTRI
Arranged by ELLIOT DEL BORGO

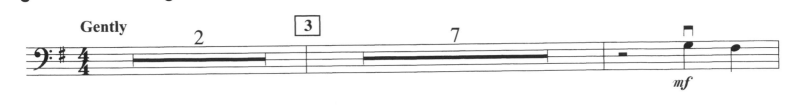

00868023

APOLLO 13

(End Credits)

By JAMES HORNER
Arranged by ELLIOT DEL BORGO

STRING BASS
String Orchestra Arrangement

00868023

From **DANCES WITH WOLVES**

THE JOHN DUNBAR THEME

STRING BASS
String Orchestra Arrangement

By JOHN BARRY
Arranged by ELLIOT DEL BORGO

THEME FROM E.T.

(The Extra-Terrestrial)

STRING BASS
String Orchestra Arrangement

Music by JOHN WILLIAMS
Arranged by ELLIOT DEL BORGO

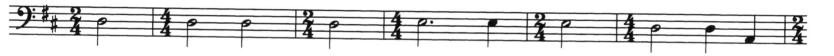

From the Universal Motion Picture JURASSIC PARK

THEME FROM "JURASSIC PARK"

STRING BASS
String Orchestra Arrangement

Composed by JOHN WILLIAMS
Arranged by ELLIOT DEL BORGO

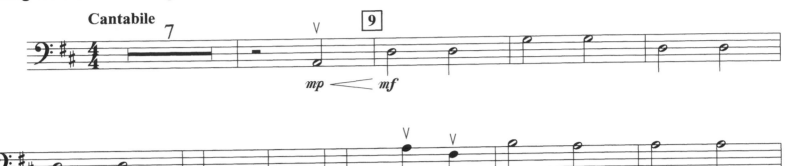

THE MAN FROM SNOWY RIVER
(Main Title Theme)

STRING BASS
String Orchestra Arrangement

By BRUCE ROWLAND
Arranged by ELLIOT DEL BORGO

00868023

From the Paramount Motion Picture MISSION: IMPOSSIBLE

MISSION: IMPOSSIBLE THEME

STRING BASS
String Orchestra Arrangement

By LALO SCHIFRIN
Arranged by ELLIOT DEL BORGO

RAIDERS MARCH

STRING BASS
String Orchestra Arrangement

Music by JOHN WILLIAMS
Arranged by ELLIOT DEL BORGO

00868023

From AN AMERICAN TAIL

SOMEWHERE OUT THERE

STRING BASS
String Orchestra Arrangement

Words and Music by JAMES HORNER,
BARRY MANN and CYNTHIA WEIL
Arranged by ELLIOT DEL BORGO

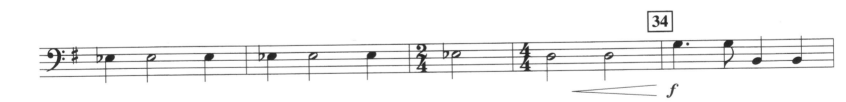

MCA MUSIC PUBLISHING

00868023

STAR TREK® THE MOTION PICTURE

STRING BASS
String Orchestra Arrangement

Music by JERRY GOLDSMITH
Arranged by ELLIOT DEL BORGO